Breakfast with God

by

Paul L. Jakes, Jr.

Heart Thoughts Publishing
Floyds Knobs, IN

Unless otherwise indicated, the Scriptures quoted are taken from the Authorized King James Version of the Bible.

Copyright © 2013 by Paul L. Jakes, Jr.

All rights reserved. This book or any portion thereof may not be reproduced or used in any manner whatsoever without the express written permission of the publisher except for the use of brief quotations in a book review.

Printed in the United States of America

First Printing, 2013

ISBN-13: 978-1492113485
ISBN-10: 1492113484

LCCN: 2013947663

Heart Thoughts Publishing
P.O. Box 536
Floyds Knobs, IN 47119

Dedication

I dedicate this book to my mother, Lorraine Jakes, and late father, Rev. Paul L. Jakes, Sr., who helped me become the man of faith that I am today. I also dedicate this to my younger brother, Pastor Martin L. Jakes, Sr., Pastor of Light of the World Church International in Atlanta Georgia, who sparked this drive to write and to Elder Evan Simmons who said, "A disciplined life makes all the difference."

A special thank you to my New Tabernacle of Faith Baptist Church family in Chicago, IL.

Thanks to my publishers, Vanessa Collins and Arlene Bell; my proofreader, Minister Aretha Tatum; Rev. Dr. Kwame John R. Porter who encouraged me to write a book; and Pastor Paul A. Southerland Ph.D., a scholar and graduate from the University of Chicago, who listened daily with a Theologian's Ear.

Special thanks to my prayer partners Dr. Rogers Jackson, Bishop Louis Clark, and Dr. Alberto Rosa.

Special thanks to my Pastor Caliph Wyatt who gave me my first job at Bethany Garfield Park Hospital during the summer to get money for college. I will always be grateful for his friendship. Rev. Wyatt is the dynamic pastor of Monroe Baptist Church, in Bellwood Illinois.

Ministers Lydia and Rosa Jiggetts provided help and encouragement while I attended Virginia Union School of Theology. Many papers were typed during that time by Minister Lydia Jiggetts and I will always be grateful. Moreover, these women of God provided additional encouragement by getting Rita Jackson, a professional seamstress, to make several robes that I wore each Sunday delivering God's Word to my congregation on Chicago's Westside.

Daily conversations with former Congressman Gus Savage, award-winning journalist, newspaper publisher, and former neighbor and my employer as his District Administrator, made all the difference in critical thinking and leadership development.

I also dedicate this book to one of the best oratorical speakers that I have heard since Dr. Martin Luther King, Jr. He is better known as TNT, Attorney Thomas N. Todd, former full Law Professor at the University of Chicago and former President of the Southern Christian Leadership Conference - Chicago Chapter, and former National President of Operation P.U.S.H. On a weekly basis, I was taught how to read behind the lines of the newspapers to address the needs of God's people and to minister to their bodies, minds and spirits.

To Channel 2 former news anchorman, John Davis, who provides public relations services and is the Master of Ceremonies par excellence for most of our major events. He has taught me how subliminal statements are just as powerful as rocks thrown.

To my friend, Ghingo W. Brooks, former President of Malcolm X College who taught me how important it is to document everything and take good notes in meetings. President Brooks also taught me the importance in delegating responsibilities and following up with the team to make sure that the job is properly done.

I also dedicate this book to Evangelist Synita B. Capler, director of Shift Ministries, who helped re-type and edit many papers at Northern Baptist Theological Seminary in Lombard Illinois. For several years she served as secretary for the Christian Council on Urban Affairs providing technical help, along with her daughter Lynita Capler.

To my friend and brother in the Lord, ordained deacon Dr. Danny K. Davis, who serves as U.S. Congressman for the seventh district in Chicago, Illinois. Every now and then we will sing a song together and afterwards Dr. Davis would tell me the secrets of writing. He would say his commitment to writing is to get up at 3:00 a.m. and write. What a blessing he has been in my life down through the years.

To Attorney Craig Tobin, an excellent legal voice for justice in the court system who has helped many people. He has been a friend who shares and cares.

To Attorney James Montgomery, a man of great wisdom, influence, and favor. Through his law firm and his generosity, he provided me a scholarship to advance my Theological education at Northern Baptist Seminary. I will always be grateful for his support of my ministry.

To Apostle John Eckhardt, an author of over 50 books, who has inspired me down through the years with his powerful teaching on television. Now, a personal friend, who has encouraged me to write and provide leadership workshops to help other pastors and leaders. Through Pastor Eckhardt's help, we have provided some informative Christian education sessions by the grace of God. Moreover, I thank Apostle Eckhardt for helping to get the word out about this book all over the world.

Table of Contents

Introduction 9
Day 1 – Theme: Separate unto Him 11
Day 2 – Theme: Jesus Paid It All 13
Day 3 - Theme: Faith in Action 15
Day 4 – Theme: Be Kingdom of God Minded 17
Day 5 – Theme: I'll Guide Thee Home 19
Day 6 - Theme: Break the Fear Threshold 21
Day 7 – Theme: Turn the World Right Side Up 23
Day 8 – Theme: The Word Became Flesh 25
Day 9 – Theme: David Spares Saul's Life 27
Day 10 – Theme: Being Obedient to God 29
Day 11 - Theme: Lord Govern My Footsteps 33
Day 12 – Theme: Giving that Glorifies God 35
Day 13 – Theme: Winning the World for Christ 37
Day 14 – Theme - God's Living Letters 39
Day 15 – Theme: Gifts that Build the Church 41
Day 16 – Theme: A Better Way to Live 43
Day 17 – Theme: Justified by Faith in Christ (Declared innocent by Faith in God) 45
Day 18 – Theme: One in the Spirit 47
Day 19 – Theme: Because Jesus Lives, We Live 49
Day 20 – Theme: The Believer's Adoption and Inheritance 51
Day 21 – Theme: Family of God 53
Day 22 – Theme: Put Your Name in the Promise 55
Day 23 – Theme: Choose An Obedient Life 57
Day 24 – Theme: When the Mouth Speaks, the Mind Listens .. 59
Day 25 – Theme: Good News! 61
Day 26 – Theme: Sitting on the Edge of His Seat 63
Day 27 – Theme: Be Holy 65
Day 28 – Theme: Evidence of Divine Residence 67
Day 29 – Theme: Trust the Great Physician 69
Day 30 – Theme: Unlock the Mysteries 71

Introduction

All good things come from the Lord.

It is my hope that the efforts of providing these meditations will help the lives of those who read them. The concept of writing this book of meditations was watered first by my brother, Martin Jakes, who is a pastor in Atlanta, Georgia. On New Year's Day, a few years ago, he shared with me that the Lord wanted me to write a book. Further watering came when I was encouraged by Elder Evan Simmons, who lives in Washington D.C., to do a daily diary. Elder Simmons has done major leadership conferences in Chicago. He shared that this level of discipline would improve my spiritual walk with God, and it did. This process helped me to reflect upon my days, weeks, months and years.

Doing your own daily devotion will strengthen your resolve to be used for God's glory each and every day. Try it and see how it will make your spiritual life more complete.

Day 1 – Theme: Separate unto Him

Scripture: "And the LORD shall guide thee continually, and satisfy thy soul in drought, and make fat thy bones: and thou shalt be like a watered garden, and like a spring of water, whose waters fail not." Isaiah 58:11

Hymn: "Still Away to Jesus"

Thought for Today:

We as Christians have hang-ups due to sin. Like Israel's leaders, we don't keep a time of worship and devotion. We get so busy with our life that we lay aside the real life through Jesus Christ. Right now God is calling His church to separate ourselves from the day to day routine and get closer to Him. Isaiah 58:6 (KJV) says it this way: "Is not this the fast that I have chosen? to loose the bands of wickedness, to undo the heavy burdens, and to let the oppressed go free, and that ye break every yoke?" The fast that God is talking about has very little to do with simply going without food. It is a life style. It is a commitment to saying that I am breaking the hold of wickedness on my life. I am taking no phone calls because I am listening to God. I am turning off the television, and I will turn on teaching tapes. I will put down magazines and pick up the Bible. Instead of sitting at my desk, I will fall down on my knees and pray that God will free me of my bondage and then, when I am free, I will pray for my family, church and community as well. I will pray that no blockers keep me from what the Lord has for me.

Prayer:

Dear Lord,

We are thankful that You came to a world that knew You not. But for those who receive, You shall call them Sons and Daughters of God. Therefore, we will sanctify (separate) ourselves to You and be grateful that You have given us wisdom to know who to fellowship with and who not. In Jesus' name we pray, Amen.

Reflections:

_____

_____

_____

_____

_____

_____

_____

_____

_____

_____

_____

_____

_____

Day 2 – Theme: Jesus Paid It All

Scripture: "As His divine power has given to us all things that pertain to life and godliness, through the knowledge of Him who called us by glory and virtue," 2 Peter 1:3 (NKJV)

Hymn: "Jesus is All the World to Me"

Thought for Today:

Glory is our response in tribulation. Therefore as Christians we are to pursue the wisdom of God, the plan of God, and the Word of God. This pleases God (2 Peter 1:17-18). God showed His pleasure with Jesus who became the sacrifice for humanity and overcame temptation. Jesus was the only one who could fulfill prophecy and be the true "Light of the World" (2 Peter 1:19).

Like others who have traveled this road of ministry, I know the fruitfulness of our Lord, and that God will do anything for me. I have seen His mighty acts of love providing for me out of His riches in glory (2 Peter 1: 8). I thank God for all He has done for me. I raise my hands in praise to God for He keeps on blessing me.

Prayer:
Dear Lord,
Every day we find ourselves facing the cost for our sins, unbelief, and temptations. You prophetically made a way for us when our backs were up against the wall. Now that You have paid the bill for my redemption, let me walk each day with You. You are my portion and remedy for everything I go through and I thank You for Your faithfulness. In Jesus' name we pray, Amen.

Reflections:

Day 3 - Theme: Faith in Action

Scripture: "And Samuel took a sucking lamb, and offered *it for* a burnt offering wholly unto the LORD: and Samuel cried unto the LORD for Israel; and the LORD heard him." 1 Samuel 7:9

Hymn: "A Charge to Keep I Have"

Thought for Today:

One of the commands from the Lord to the children of Israel was to draw water and pour it out before the Lord (1 Samuel 7:6). They were also directed to fast for that day and to admit their wrong against the Lord. Water is often used to symbolize the Holy Spirit. The pouring out of water on the ground also symbolizes our utter helplessness (2 Samuel 14:14). It is profoundly revealed in the Bible that repentance is a must for revival to take place with sinful man. All of us are prodigal sons who need to be restored unto our father (Luke 15:23-24). Restoration is a call and response quality, for Jesus said, "We must first deny ourselves daily and follow Him" (Luke 9:23).

Therefore, restoration comes from a disciplined life following the teachings of Jesus and not just following laws that we so often are not able to keep (Colossians 2:14-16). The song writer wrote "Jesus paid it all, all to Him I owe."

Prayer:
Dear God,
Accept our petition before Your mercy seat. Help us to forgive that we can be forgiven. In Jesus' name we pray, Amen.

Reflections:

Day 4 – Theme: Be Kingdom of God Minded

Scripture: "Who hath delivered us from the power of darkness, and hath translated *us* into the kingdom of his dear Son" Colossians 1:13

Hymn: "I Love Thy Kingdom, Lord"

Thought for Today:

Apostle Paul, in his missionary journey to the east, comforts and gives thanks to God for the churches of Ephesus, Colosse, and Philippians. Paul encourages them to be kingdom minded. He calls for them to live a Christ-like life, assuring them that they will be strengthened with all power (Philippians 1:9-11). It seems to me that our aim in life should be to please God and when we do, we become a part of the royal family with all benefits. So, I am convinced that the world we wake up into is not the ultimate world. The ultimate world happens when we move from the natural to the supernatural, and this can happen without dying naturally. This happens when we put to death the things of this world and walk with Jesus as Lord of our lives. As Colossians 1:13 states, "who hath delivered us from the power of darkness, and hath translated us into the kingdom of his dear Son." Paul further states that we all are heirs to the kingdom of God (Colossians 1:16).

Prayer:
Dear God,
Help us use our time wisely that no grass grows up under our feet. For I am older now, and the days are moving faster. Bless my extended days to maximize the work for the kingdom of God. Bless my family and friends. In Jesus' name we pray, Amen.

Breakfast with God

Reflections:

Day 5 – Theme: I'll Guide Thee Home

Scripture: "In whom we have boldness and access with confidence by the faith of him." Ephesians 3:12

Hymn: "Holy Spirit, Faithful Guide"

Thought for Today:

Preaching is a statement of faith that shows that we are more than conquerors through Jesus Christ. Paul, in this epistle, writes about the revelation of the mysteries of Christ (Ephesians 3:3-4).

All that believe in Jesus Christ are new creatures in Him. God does not discriminate (Ephesians 3:6). Paul reveals that God has used him since his conversion, even facilitating a personal study with him for over three years. Paul meets and shares with Peter, for fifteen days, the working of the Holy Spirit in his life (Galatians 1:18).

Even though Paul made it to Peter, his journey did not end there. Paul was to go where the Spirit led him. Paul's mission helped the Gentiles to know Jesus Christ as their Lord. What pain our Savior endured for all men and women to be rescued from our sins (John 3:16)! Paul knew that our goal is not to seek man's approval but God's (Romans 4:25). Paul's pursuit was to be in the will of God knowing that through Jesus that we are victors, conquerors in Him (Romans 8:37).

Prayer:

Given to me by Robert in Nashville TN.

Lord, keep us faithful to Your Word. Although at times we might rephrase, help us never to twist its truth to justify our selfish ways. We must align ourselves with the Bible and never try to align the Bible to ourselves. In Jesus' name we pray, Amen.

Reflections:

Day 6 - Theme: Break the Fear Threshold

Scripture: "So that we may boldly say, The Lord *is* my helper, and I will not fear what man shall do unto me." Hebrews 13:6

Hymn: "He Leadeth Me"

Thought for Today

Our testimonies are statements of faith echoed to other believers. It displays, in living color, how you trusted God even when you could not see your way. Hebrews 11:1 says, "Now faith is the substance of things hoped for and the evidence of things not seen." So to access the manifold blessings of God we must overcome our fears. Psalms 27: 1 states, "The Lord is of my light and my salvation; whom shall I fear? The Lord is the strength of my life; of whom shall I be afraid?"

In this economy many are wondering how they are going to survive. Don't believe the hype by the enemy. Trust God! Matthew 6:25 expresses not to worry about these things in life. Manifestations will happen soon. Expect it!

Prayer:
Dear God,
I know that you are bigger than any financial cliff. I feel like I am in the valley. So please, won't you open the windows of heaven, and send out a ladder that I might climb out of the valley, up past my cliffs, to the peaks of heaven, where the blessed windows are open awaiting me. In Jesus' name we pray, Amen.

Reflections:

Day 7 – Theme: Turn the World Right Side Up

Scripture: "But made himself of no reputation, and took upon him the form of a servant, and was made in the likeness of men" Philippians 2:7

Hymns: "Send the Light"

Thought for Today:

Both Christ's humanity and divinity are key for our salvation. All through the Bible are reports of our sins that had left us helpless, lost and unable to save ourselves. Only God could provide a sacrifice to cover our sins. Philippians 2:8 tells us that Jesus, being found in fashion as a man, humbled himself and became obedient unto death, even the death of the cross. Therefore, it is through our faith that we can be born again. We can be saved by His grace and mercy. When Adam and Eve sinned they were removed from the immediate presence of God.

Our involvement and habits should glorify God as children of His house. As the song tells us "God loves us all; red, yellow, brown, black or white. All are precious in His sight." Galatians 4:5 says it like this, "To redeem them that were under the law, that we might receive the adoption of sons." Jesus knew that there were souls to rescue and save. So He took on the form of man and brought light into the world. According to Philippians 2:15, God desires that we are blameless and harmless, the sons of God, without rebuke, in the midst of crooked and perverse nation, among whom we shine as lights in the world. Through faith we can turn this world "right side up;" for John 14:12 says, "He that believeth on me, the works that I do shall he do also, and greater works than these shall he do, because I go unto my Father."

Jesus turned the world right side up:
- Up from moral crises to moral authority in Christ.
- Up from darkness into the marvelous light.
- Up from life's shadows to the sweet dawn of God's daylight.
- Up from pain and sorrow to a new morning burden free and pain free through Christ.
- Up from envy, jealousy, strife, back biting, lying, recklessness, deceit, rage, and cursing to the generation of Faith.

Prayer:
Dear Lord,

Joy floods my soul when I think how You took on the form of man and surrendered Yourself as the perfect sacrifice. The only way I can thank You is to love someone else and by going the extra distance to help someone in need. I'll go, Lord I'll go. If You need somebody, here am I dear Lord, send me. In Jesus' name we pray, Amen.

Reflections:

_____

_____

_____

_____

_____

_____

_____

Day 8 – Theme: The Word Became Flesh

Scripture: "And the Word was made flesh, and dwelt among us, (and we beheld his glory, the glory as of the only begotten of the Father,) full of grace and truth." John 1:14

Hymn: "Pass Me Not, O Gentle Savior"

Thought for Today:

Divine enlightment is important to understanding Jesus the great revelator. It is just like wearing glasses. If the glasses do not match your specific prescription, you will not be able to see clearly. John the Baptist was not the light but was used to point toward the light for all men to see. John realized that he must decrease but Jesus must increase (John 3:30). Jesus came to give light to all men not just for the Jews.

Jesus' message was unlimited; it embraced the entire world. This evidence was manifested at the day of Pentecost where He poured out His spirit on all in the Upper Room. Through our faith in Jesus Christ, His dying on the cross and His resurrection, we not only have salvation but also the Holy Spirit that leads us into all truths.

I have looked at many blind people and they have special gifts to hear more effectively. However, one gift that I am awed by is the gift to take their hands and feel the face of a person and determine how they look to them.

We, too, are blind seeking to know God's face. But I believe that we can see God by looking at His creation. We see Him in the sky, the Grand Cannon, the seas that flow to the great oceans, and the springs that sprout up in the middle of the desert. That is God lighting the way for the entire world to know Him better.

Prayer:
Dear God,
    Help our spiritual sight that we will not walk blindly in this world. Be the lighthouse that shines brightly as we sail on the waves of life. In Jesus' name we pray, Amen.

Reflections:

Day 9 – Theme: David Spares Saul's Life

Scripture: "Recompense to no man evil for evil. Provide things honest in the sight of all men." Romans 12:17

Hymn: "Am I A Soldier of the Cross"

Thought for Today:

The anointing of God is an opportunity to participate in the service of the Lord. Man looks on the outward parts, but God looks at the heart, much like He did with David. Deuteronomy 30:6 says; "and the Lord thy God will circumcise thine heart, and the heart of thy seed." It is easy to understand why God said that David was a man after His own heart. Life is empty without obedience to God. David was amazing because he allowed God to order his steps. Psalms 145: 1-21 gives us all a glimpse of David's heart. Verse 8 seems to wrap it up in these words; "The Lord is gracious, and full of compassion; slow to anger, and of great mercy."

Maybe that is what is on the mind of David when he had the opportunity to kill King Saul. It takes great courage to have your enemy in a vulnerable position and not defeat him. For David showed great honor to the King and controlled his anger. 1 Samuel 26:7-9 tells us that David spared King Saul's life and leaves the chastisement to God.

A great preacher once said that vengeance has nothing to do with hate but the love of justice. He further said to expect the favor of God. You don't have to fight your own battle. All God wants us to do is to stay in love. The question is before us daily, do we love the Lord enough to obey Him?

Prayer:

Dear God,

    I want to thank you for my deliverance, for the days have been long. Although I have experienced cruel crushing blows, you are my carefree zone, a way out of no way and a brighter day ahead. In Jesus' name we pray, Amen.

Reflections:

_____

_____

_____

_____

_____

_____

_____

_____

_____

_____

_____

_____

_____

_____

Day 10 – Theme: Being Obedient to God

Scripture: "And Samuel said, Hath the LORD *as great* delight in burnt offerings and sacrifices, as in obeying the voice of the LORD? Behold, to obey *is* better than sacrifice, *and* to hearken than the fat of rams." 1 Samuel 15:22

Hymn: "Have Thine Own Way, Lord"

Thought for Today:

King Saul's failure as a king was centered on his lack of complete obedience to God. South of Israel, toward Egypt, dwelt the Amalekites, a semi-nomadic desert tribe. They were so wicked that God said they must be destroyed. They were so bad that there was no hope that they would ever repent for their sins. So God told Saul to utterly destroy them, including all of their possessions. It was the judgment of God, and nothing was to be spared. But Saul spared Agag, the king, and the best of the sheep, and of the oxen, and of the fatlings, and the lambs, and all that was good, and would not utterly destroy them: but everything that was vile and refuse, that they destroyed utterly (1 Samuel 15:9).

Choosing to be obedient and live victorious by the power of God is strength, not a weakness. It should never be our desire to grieve God or His servant but to follow His every command and be loyal so that we will be established forever in God's presence.

In 1780 America suffered a number of setbacks. In the south, the British had routed the army of General Gates. In New England, the treason of Benedict Arnold almost succeeded in losing West Point to the British. And, by the end of the year, the financing of the military effort was so haphazard and uncertain that it seemed almost impossible to carry on the struggle for freedom. Then, in January, 1781, mutiny developed among the troops. Many had received no pay for months, and provisions were woefully inadequate. Consequently, one thousand men marched to Philadelphia to present their complaints to Congress.

There was danger that the mutiny would sweep through the entire army, in which case any hope for victory would be gone. Sir Henry Clinton, the British general in New York, was confident that the mutinous would join his forces, and he sent messengers to them with an appealing offer. To his great surprise it was rejected as being contemptuous. The loyalty of these men was not for sale. Soon their grievances were settled and victory accrued.

Similarly, God wants commitment and devotion, and, most of all, strength to walk away from the bribes of the enemy. God wants Godly action, for once you have put on Godly clothing then Godly actions must follow in the army of the Lord.

The song writer says, "Take my life and let it be consecrated, Lord to thee; Take my feet, and let them be swift and beautiful for thee; Take my silver and gold, not a mite with I withhold; Take my will and make it thine, It shall be no longer mine; Take my heart, it shall be thy royal throne, it shall be thy royal throne."

Prayer:
Dear God,
    Although I may face cold situations, please give me Your spiritual covering that I may never freeze or feel the winds of circumstances. I want the moment of warmth

knowing that You will never pass me by. In Jesus' name we pray, Amen.

Reflections:

Reflections:

Day 11 - Theme: Lord Govern My Footsteps

Scripture: "And the LORD said unto Samuel, Hearken unto the voice of the people in all that they say unto thee: for they have not rejected thee, but they have rejected me, that I should not reign over them. According to all the works which they have done since the day that I brought them up out of Egypt even unto this day, wherewith they have forsaken me, and served other gods, so do they also unto thee." 1 Samuel 8:7-8

Hymn: "Great Is Thy Faithfulness"

Thought for Today:

The children of Israel used any excuse they could to justify having a king like the other nations had. The counsel of Elders ignores Samuel's counsel. The Elders pointed out that Samuel's sons, Joel and Abiah, were not so exemplary. As appointed Judges over Israel in Beersheba, they took bribes, and perverted judgment (1 Samuel 8:3).

God directed Samuel to do as they had requested for they had not rejected him but God. The appointment of Saul proved over time to be a decision that was made without God as he became stuck on himself rather than stuck on God.

The book of James says that if any of you lack wisdom ask of God. How can one reign correctly without God? It is clear to me that all Saul had to do was to ask God for guidance, but he did not. He thought that the victories were because of him and not God's intervention. In Samuel 16:14 it says that the Spirit of the Lord had rejected him, but because he had discarded God, believing he no longer needed Him. There is a song that says, "I need you, you are all I need." Unless we come to the realization that our strength, our victories, our pursuit for happiness, and all of our help comes from the Lord, we will fail every time. If we humble ourselves before God, He will elevate us.

We must refrain from self congratulations and give all the glory to God. Be kind to all people, because one can be up today and down tomorrow. Self idolatry must be destroyed or it will destroy you, like it did with King Saul. As we lift up Jesus Christ, the Son of God, and put Satan behind us, we are on the path of righteousness. The devil can't make you do anything. Why? Because God the Father, God the Son, and God the Holy Spirit is more powerful than Satan, and Satan was defeated at the cross through the blood of Jesus and His resurrection.

Prayer:
Dear God,
   Let me live a life with a higher code of ethics, and let the Word of God govern my footsteps. Let me not disregard Your Word. Seize me, regenerate me, and never dismiss me from Your grace. In Jesus' name we pray, Amen.

Reflections:

_____

_____

_____

_____

_____

Day 12 – Theme: Giving that Glorifies God

Scripture: "Every man according as he purposeth in his heart, *so let him give*; not grudgingly, or of necessity: for God loveth a cheerful giver." 2 Corinthians 9:7

Hymn: "Praise God From Whom All Blessings Flow"

Thought for Today:

A dear friend of mine, who served as a county police officer, gave up her career to take care of her son who was hit by a car and paralyzed for the rest of his life. She started a home day care that would allow her to bring in some resources to make a livelihood and take care of her son at the same time. However, the real point of this story is that she did it voluntarily, cheerfully, and lovingly.

Sacrifice will produce the things inside of you that will bring a harvest. 2 Corinthians 9:6-7 says it like this: "But this I say, He which soweth sparingly shall reap sparingly; and he which soweth bountifully shall reap also bountifully. Every man according as he purposed in his heart, so let him give; not grudgingly, or of necessity; for God loveth a cheerful giver."

Jesus taught us that the position of strength is in service. The church of Macedonia gave out of its poverty, and Paul says that the grace of God was with them. Grace comes from one being obedient to God's will, and strength comes from identified Christian character. Our prayer is that the Lord will help us respond to the needs of others and be gracious and good.

Prayer:
Dear God,
    We expect Your blessings, covering, influence, prosperity, protection, and promise. No matter what season we may be in, a new day is coming. In Jesus' name we pray, Amen.

Reflections:
_____
_____
_____
_____
_____
_____
_____
_____
_____
_____
_____
_____
_____
_____
_____
_____

Day 13 – Theme: Winning the World for Christ

Scripture: Now then we are ambassadors for Christ, as though God did beseech *you* by us: we pray *you* in Christ's stead, be ye reconciled to God. 2 Corinthians 5:20

Hymn: "Till the Whole World Knows"

Thought for Today:

God's grace and mercy was truly revealed when Jesus went to the cross for our sins. Romans 3:23-24 says, "for all have sinned and come short of the glory of God; being justified freely by his grace through the redemption that is in Christ Jesus." Therefore, if we believe that Jesus died and rose again for our sins we should live for Him.

I have concluded that to walk in the way of Adam is to walk in darkness, but if we are led by Jesus, He leads us to the light. I believe if we view ourselves as agents of faith, we are bound to help men see Jesus through Godly character. Verse 17 says, "If any man be in Christ he is a new creature: old things are passed away; behold, all things are become new."

New duties, new privileges, new brothers, new sisters, and new hopes are ours. We are no longer strangers and foreigners, but fellow citizens with the saints and of the household of God.

Prayer:
Dear God,
Jonah had to learn that all people belong to you. And You gave him a Word that led the city to repentance. Please give us a Word to save those that are lost in the cities that we minister, and let us never get off course. In Jesus' name we pray, Amen.

Reflections:

Day 14 – Theme - God's Living Letters

Scripture: "Ye are our epistle written in our hearts, known and read of all men" 2 Corinthians 3:2

Hymn: "Love Led Him to Calvary"

Thought for Today:

We as Christians should never forget that every day people are watching us. Therefore, realize that the only Jesus they see is in you. Jesus is not in the borrowed tomb; He has ascended to His father and sits at the right hand of God.

So our lives must be a witness, with a smile or a helping hand, that our living will not be in vain.

There is a poem, whose author is unknown, that makes this very clear:

> Men read and admire the Gospel of Christ, With His love so unfailing and true; but what do they say, and what do they think, Of the Gospel "according to you?"

> You are writing each day a letter to men; take care that the writing is true; "Tis the only Gospel that some men will read - That Gospel according to you."

So when one gives their life to Jesus because of your witness, rejoicing is in order. That person has agreed to put to death their old nature and to live victoriously for Christ.

The Gospel song writer pinned these words: "Let the life you live be a reflection of the man inside."

Prayer:
Dear God,
    Now I can see Your plan for my life. Even through my tears of grief and pain, I know You live because You live in me. In Jesus' name we pray, Amen.

Reflections:

Day 15 – Theme: Gifts that Build the Church

Scripture: "Even so ye, forasmuch as ye are zealous of spiritual *gifts*, seek that ye may excel to the edifying of the church." 1 Corinthians 14:12

Hymn: "Standing on the Promises"

Thought for Today:

On the day of Pentecost, no interpreter was needed because the church was on one accord. To those outside of the church, the words seemed unintelligent without an interpreter. In fact, Peter had to tell the people outside of the church that they were not drunk because the taverns had not opened yet.

I don't believe that Peter's explanation was to astonish or show off to others the new gift. It was to be a constant witness of harmony and pure edification and communication among the body of Christ. So maybe this is why Paul says this gift speaks not unto men, but unto God. The use of the tongue Paul had in mind was an expression of worship to God. In verses 23 and 24, Paul urges those that have the gift of prophesy to speak where hearers can understand in order not to disturb and confuse the individual. The lack of understanding can greatly affect their lives. It is clear to me that Paul understood the value of the gift of tongues, but he recognized the greater value of prophecy. The key words are edification, exhortation, comfort, cheer and counsel to the Body of Christ. It is not enough to display gifts. These gifts must have a practical and helpful effect on the lives of the Christian fellowship.

Prayer:
Dear God,
    Please give us the spirit of helps to move past the surface of ministry to the depths of doing as You did; feeding the hungry, clothing the naked, washing the feet of Your disciples, and humbling Yourself to go to the cross for our sins. In Jesus' name we pray, Amen.

Reflections:

Day 16 – Theme: A Better Way to Live

Scripture: "Charity suffereth long, *and* is kind; charity envieth not; charity vaunteth not itself, is not puffed up, Doth not behave itself unseemly, seeketh not her own, is not easily provoked, thinketh no evil" 1 Corinthians 13:4, 5

Hymn: "More Love To Thee"

Thought for Today:

Eyesight is important to help us see the communities that we live in. Legs are important to carry us from destination to destination. Arms are important for those who desire to carry things or embrace others. All that I have mentioned are parts of our body and are needed for various functions.

However, without a functioning heart in our bodies, we cannot live. It allows everything in us to move. Therefore, charity is the heart of the Body of Christ, and it gives us power to serve humanity.

James Russell Lowell sees something of this when in "The Vision of Sir Launfal" he pictures Jesus as saying to the Knight who has turned from giving to selfless sharing:

Not what we give, but what we share, For the gift without the giver is bare; Who gives himself with his alms feeds three, Himself, his hungering neighbor, and Me.

Giving may go the distance of martyrdom, but still is useless without love.

Prayer:
Dear God,

Never divorce us from your love, especially in the time of trouble, weakness, doubt, and despair. Teach us how to appreciate every blessing, every miracle, every intervention, and every act of forgiveness. In Jesus' name we pray, Amen.

Reflections:

Day 17 – Theme: Justified by Faith in Christ (Declared innocent by Faith in God)

Scripture: "I am crucified with Christ: nevertheless I live; yet not I, but Christ liveth in me: and the life which I now live in the flesh I live by the faith of the Son of God, who loved me, and gave himself for me." Galatians 2:20

Hymn: "No One Ever Cared for Me Like Jesus"

Thought for Today:

Many believers have debated the issue of law and grace. In my theological quest for truth, I have looked into the argument of Paul who, in Galatians 2:19-20, talks of dying to sin and living for God. It is clear to me that long before we could do our part, God did his part. Our only action is to let Christ occupy us for His service. God wants us to recognize His presence by having Godly characteristics. 2 Peter 1:4-9 gives reference of being changed, purged from old sins. We must never forget that we are forgiven people.

Jesus laid down His life. He was not murdered. He gave His life willingly. You can't put new wine into old wine skins. You can't put law into grace. We are righteously favored, we are righteously healed, and we are righteously redeemed. It is not because of our efforts but by what Jesus did on the cross through His shed blood.

Prayer:
Dear God,

It was Your amazing grace that saved a person like me. I have seen many dangerous times and I felt alone, but You comforted me, held my hand and brought me out of darkness into the marvelous light of Your word. In Jesus' name we pray, Amen.

Reflections:

Day 18 – Theme: One in the Spirit

Scripture: "But the manifestation of the Spirit is given to every man to profit withal." 1 Corinthians 12:7

Hymn: "We Are One in the Spirit"

Thought for Today:

Jesus reaches the world through love, redemption and peace. We too must allow our voices, our hands, our feet, and the expressions on our faces to show God's love and His divine message for the world. As I write this morning, I praise God for technology. However, this did not exist during Paul's time of ministry. But God allowed the gifts to manifest to compensate for the lack of these technical gifts. When we are on assignment from God, He provides for us and makes provision for our weaknesses so that nothing can hold us back. We even see this revealed in Acts 2:8, where the bystanders hearing the gift of tongues for the first time wondered, "And how hear we every man in our own tongue, wherein we were born?"

The Spiritual gifts are necessary even today with all of the technology that we have. Technology cannot take the place of the Holy Spirit. All wisdom, knowledge, faith, healings, miracles, prophecy, tongues and interpretations of tongues comes from God. Likewise, the church cook, the janitor, the church secretary, the preacher, the usher, the Sunday school teacher and the musician all show the purpose of the gifts and work together as one body.

Prayer:
Dear God,
Wherever You go let my footsteps follow You. As a follower of Christ, equip me with the vestment and

spiritual fortitude to make this pilgrimage as I journey to communities unknown. In Jesus' name we pray, Amen.

Reflections:

_____

_____

_____

_____

_____

_____

_____

_____

_____

_____

_____

_____

_____

_____

_____

_____

Day 19 – Theme: Because Jesus Lives, We Live

Scripture: "But thanks *be* to God, which giveth us the victory through our Lord Jesus Christ." 1 Corinthians 15:57

Hymn: "Battle Hymn of the Republic"

Thought for Today:

If Christ had not risen, how miserable life and the life after death would be. Paul says that our preaching would be in vain or empty. He questions why we would sacrifice our lives to announce Christ's death, burial, and resurrection for the redemption of man if it were not so.

Thousands of heroic martyrs died preaching not of Buddha in his grave or Mohammed in his tomb but of Jesus who rose from the dead. Even though the Greeks had a hard time accepting Paul's message of the resurrection of Christ, he won many with his conviction and broad understanding of their culture and thinking. The Apostle Paul warned them of the consequences of denial and centers the essential gospel on faith. Paul advocated that the message is true, and upon this truth is the Christian faith, a force in the world.

Prayer:
Dear God,

I thank You for another day, a day that has been coming since the beginning of the world. This day, let me hear the inner voice of God for my protection, strength and guide. For with You, God, I will live and not die, praise You and not falter, pursue holiness and not the world. In Jesus' name we pray, Amen.

Reflections:

Day 20 – Theme: The Believer's Adoption and Inheritance

Scripture: "For we are his workmanship, created in Christ Jesus unto good works, which God hath before ordained that we should walk in them." Ephesians 2:10

Hymn: "Just As I Am"

Thought for Today:

Psychiatrists, scientists, and mathematicians can't figure out why Jesus loved us enough to come from heaven to pay the price of redemption for us who had sin smeared all over us. Why they can't scientifically comprehend it is because Christ's actions on the cross were done purely out of love.

Therefore, it is our faith in Him that gives us the comprehension, joy, favor and adoption that ushers us into the presence of God. It is refreshing that His blood washes away our sin and gives us access to the Father, for God recognizes us because of Jesus' blood. Moreover, our relationship with God moves us into change as we consecrate ourselves by submitting to His purpose for our lives.

> That if thou shalt confess with thy mouth the Lord Jesus, and shalt believe in thine heart that God hath raised him from the dead, thou shalt be saved. For with the heart man believeth unto righteousness; and with the mouth confession is made unto salvation.
>
> Romans 10:9-10

Prayer:

Dear Lord,

Breathe on us and shape us according to Your will and Your way. Your grace has given us another chance to live and not die. So as we live, Lord, work on us that we can serve You better and freely magnify Your wondrous acts. Mold us and make us in Your image and likeness. In Jesus' name we pray, Amen.

Reflections:

_____

_____

_____

_____

_____

_____

_____

_____

_____

_____

_____

Day 21 – Theme: *Family of God*

Scripture: "For both he that sanctifieth and they who are sanctified *are* all of one: for which cause he is not ashamed to call them brethren." Hebrews 2:11

Hymn: "Ashamed of Jesus"

Thought for Today:

It is refreshing to know that Christ is not ashamed of us. Even with the many struggles, faults and failures that we have, Christ still calls us brethren (Hebrews 2:11).

Therefore, don't let anyone say to you that you are unworthy of kinship with royalty through Christ. Hebrews 2:17 says, "Wherefore in all things it behoved him to be made like unto *his* brethren, that he might be a merciful and faithful high priest in things *pertaining* to God, to make reconciliation for the sins of the people." This says that we must do our part to resist Satan and his temptations.

Believe what the Bible says, and read it every day. Believe that God is molding and making you each and every day. 2 Corinthians 5:21 says, "For he hath made him *to be* sin for us, who knew no sin; that we might be made the righteousness of God in him." All we have to do is live and act according to His will and God will work through our faith and His grace to make us righteous and to make us the family of God.

Prayer:
Dear God,

In You we trust. Give us courage to stand against the evil one. Show us who should be in our surroundings and separate us from those that will do us harm. In Jesus' name we pray, Amen.

Reflections:

Day 22 – Theme: Put Your Name in the Promise

Scripture: "After these things the word of the LORD came unto Abram in a vision, saying, Fear not, Abram: I *am* thy shield, *and* thy exceeding great reward." Genesis 15:1

Hymn: "Standing on the Promises of God"

Thought for Today:

I have learned through Abraham that we should never go by what we see but what we feel on the inside. For insight comes from the Word of God.

The Holy Scripture is the wisdom of God. God told Abraham that the children of Israel would spend four hundred years in a foreign land, which was Egypt, before they would get to Canaan, the Promised Land. Even though they had to fight many battles, the promise of the covenant was fulfilled. Abraham was one hundred and Sarah was ninety before Isaac was born, but it happened.

Sometimes we may feel like Abraham. We may not see growth in a certain area, but we must remain faithful and know that whatever God has said will happen at the right time. I know that God has a perfect plan, and victory shall be ours. Just like He did in Joshua 12:7-24, we shall possess the land and be victorious.

Prayer:

Dear God,

Open our eyes that we may see the glory of Your salvation. Thank You for never leaving us nor forsaking us, and always encouraging us. Looking unto the author and finisher of our faith; who for the joy that was set before Him endured the cross, despising the shame, and is set down at the right hand of the throne of God (Hebrews 12:2). In Jesus' name we pray, Amen.

Reflections:

Day 23 – Theme: *Choose An Obedient Life*

Scripture: "I call heaven and earth to record this day against you, *that* I have set before you life and death, blessing and cursing: therefore choose life, that both thou and thy seed may live." Deuteronomy 30:19

Hymn: "Count on Me"

Thought for Today:

Idol worship should never be mixed with true worship to God. However, that is exactly what the northern kingdom of Israel did. Even though they had been warned by the prophet of God, their fleshly appetites were given free reign. All sense of decency was lost, resulting in reckless living. They did not help the poor; they disregarded the words of the prophet and gave no witness to the truth.

2 Kings 17:5 says, "Then the king of Assyria came up throughout all the land, and went up to Samaria, and besieged it three years." But instead of calling on God for their deliverance they called on Egypt. This is strange because that is the country that had enslaved them for years, and they were only delivered by God through the leadership of Moses. So the end result was that Egypt delivers them but turned around and enslaved them again.

Exodus 3:17 shows us that God had promised them a land flowing with milk and honey. But that freedom was not to depend on others but God Himself. God will not continue to favor corruption and dissolute people. Isaiah 10:5-6 points out that the children of Israel fell not to the might of other kingdoms but by their lack of faithfulness. Therefore, we should remain faithful and committed to God only, forever.

Prayer:
Dear God,
    Accept our petition before thy mercy seat. Help us to forgive that we can be forgiven. In Jesus' name we pray, Amen.

Reflections:

Day 24 – Theme: When the Mouth Speaks, the Mind Listens

Scripture: "The Lord is on my side, I will not fear." Psalms 118:6

Hymn: "God Will Take Care of You"

Thought for Today:

This division of Psalms is the Hallel. Families sang these songs on the night of the Passover and at the beginning of the meal. It was thought that these must have been the hymns that Jesus and His disciples sang at the Last Supper (Matthew 26:30).

What you hear is what you will believe. So even if you are not convinced, just keep on saying it or singing it, and you will receive it. Cast down those fearful imaginations and every thought that is contrary to the promises of God (2 Corinthians 10:5). Keep the Word of God in your thoughts and on your lips. Know that faith grows for the believer in Christ.

Prayer:

Dear God,

Helping family and friends often pulls on my inner being as I am trying to make decisions for my future this year. Do I sit idle and do little? Do I fear the people that I love? No! As for me and my house, we will serve the Lord. The habits and practices of yesterday will diminish as You guide my footsteps each day. Please help me in my spiritual growth. In Jesus' name we pray, Amen.

Reflections:

Day 25 – Theme: Good News!

Scripture: "And it shall come to pass in that day, *that* his burden shall be taken away from off thy shoulder, and his yoke from off thy neck, and the yoke shall be destroyed because of the anointing." Isaiah 10:27

Hymn: "Ain't that Good News"

Thought for Today:

The devil has been using men and women, since the fall of man, as a pack of mules. He has clamped his yoke around their necks and burdened them down with sin, sickness, failure, poverty, and every other weight possible. However, the good news is that when Christ redeemed us on Calvary, he broke the yoke and gave us a new lease on life.

In Isaiah 6:8, the prophet shows us how we should respond to God's call and new freedom. Isaiah said, "I have heard the voice of the Lord, saying who shall I send, and who will go for us? Then said I, Here am I: send me."

It is my theological thought that when God has freed us, we should respond responsibly to life's responsibility. As Christians, we should know that Christ was hung up for our hang ups.

- Sin gave me rain but God gave me sunshine.
- Sin gave me misery but God gave me a miracle.
- Sin gave me darkness but God gave me light.
- Sin gave me curse but God gave me comfort.
- Sin gave me loss but God gave me victory.
- Sin gave me sadness but God gave me joy.
- Sin gave me failure but God gave me triumph.

- Sin gave me pain but God gave me perfect health.
- Sin gave me frustration but God gave me favor.
- Sin gave me a yoke but God gave me a redeemer.

Romans 5:1-5 gives testimony to how each experience that the enemy shoves at us works in the long run for our good if we faint not.

Prayer:
Dear God,

Save the city. The pill of sin is everywhere, and people are making that which is right to be wrong. Make us strong in our faith to just say no to sin's intoxicating drug. In Jesus' name we pray, Amen.

Reflections:

Day 26 – Theme: *Sitting on the Edge of His Seat*

Scripture: "And I will shew wonders in heaven above, and signs in the earth beneath; blood, and fire, and vapour of smoke: The sun shall be turned into darkness, and the moon into blood, before that great and notable day of the Lord come." Acts 2:19-20

Hymn: "Beyond the Sunset"

Thought for Today:

My parents would tell me, as a child, that the day would come when high skyscrapers would not stand anymore. It became increasingly clear that the occurrence of the attack on the World Trade Center was evidence of their words being true. Flipping through magazines and newspapers also shows photos from around the world where buildings are being destroyed and lives are being taken as a result of wars.

In Acts 2:17-20 the amazing sermon of Peter explains the fulfillment of prophecy; that sons and daughters shall prophesy and that visions and dreams shall manifest. Moreover, verses 19 and 20 states: "And I will shew wonders in heaven above, and signs in the earth beneath; blood, and fire, and vapour of smoke: The sun shall be turned into darkness, and the moon into blood, before that great and notable day of the Lord come."

What this revelation of Peter says to me is that we, as God's people, must be ready to do our due diligence to bring more souls into the Kingdom of God before it is too late. Local churches must begin praying for people in the community and loving them into spiritual health. Moreover, God will help us to break down the barriers that divide us, so that languages or cultures will not be a hindrance. God will facilitate ways to get people in our presence and allow them to hear the Word of God.

Prayer:
Dear God,
　　We pray for spiritual health in our communities. We pray against toxic communities of hate, violence and deceit. We will look to Jesus, the Author and Finisher of our faith! In Jesus' name we pray, Amen.

Reflections:

Day 27 – Theme: Be Holy

Scripture: "But as he which hath called you is holy, so be ye holy in all manner of conversation." 1 Peter 1:15

Hymn: "Holy, Holy, Holy, Lord God Almighty"

Thought for Today:

As a representative of God, living a holy life is imperative because the only Jesus that some people will see is the Jesus in us. Therefore, obedience to Him is the substance that gives us power to stand in the midst of pressure.

As cream separates from milk and rises to the top, so must we in our daily lives rise in our consciousness to walk and live like Christ.

Prayer

Dear God,

Be the thermostat in our lives that we can rise with You and not of our own power. Let all power and strength come from You alone. In Jesus' name we pray, Amen.

Reflections:

Day 28 – Theme: *Evidence of Divine Residence*

Scripture: "Whosoever believeth that Jesus is the Christ is born of God: and every one that loveth him that begat loveth him also that is begotten of him...For whatsoever is born of God overcometh the world: and this is the victory that overcometh the world, *even* our faith." 1 John 5:1, 4

Hymn: "Blessed Assurance"

Thought for Today:

Yesterday I went to court with a friend. I observed the judge question over a dozen people that stood before him. He asked, "Do you have evidence that you have insurance?" For it was not enough to say, "I have insurance," but it was necessary to show proof. That proof was important to show that they had insurance coverage at the time the accident occurred. Prevaricating to the judge would only put one in jail, but having proof of insurance would set them free.

Well, God has provided, through His Son Jesus, something better than insurance. He has given us His blessed assurance through faith in Him. Our proof is in the Holy Bible in 1 John 5:1: "Whosoever believeth that Jesus is the Christ is born of God: and every one that loveth him that begat loveth him also that is begotten of him." So you and I must let the life we live be a reflection of the Man inside.

Prayer:
Dear God,
 I am still looking at the ripples in the water. I feel You coming closer and closer to my heart. So let me walk and not be weary for You are my comfort before and after the storm. In Jesus' name we pray, Amen.

Reflections:

Day 29 – Theme: Trust the Great Physician

Scripture: "My son, attend to my words; incline thine ear unto my sayings. Let them not depart from thine eyes; keep them in the midst of thine heart. For they *are* life unto those that find them, and health to all their flesh. Keep thy heart with all diligence; for out of it *are* the issues of life." Proverbs 4:20-23

Hymn: "Trusting Jesus"

Thought for Today:

When I was young and visited my grandparents' home overnight, I was given specific instructions by my grandmother. She instructed me to ask for what I wanted and to not get it without permission. Nevertheless, I would sneak and get those delicious homemade cookies.

I thought I was so good at sneaking cookies that I tried it at home, which resulted in me falling off a chair and cutting my leg so badly that I needed stitches. If I had listened to my grandmother and yielded to her instructions I would have avoided this dangerous accident.

This lesson says if we live wisely and hear the instructions given us, we will experience health in our spirits and our bodies. Romans 10:17 tells us that faith comes by hearing and hearing by the Word of God.

Prayer

Dear Lord,

Help us to hear the Holy Spirit and watch where we go and what we do. In Jesus' name we pray, Amen.

Reflections:

Day 30 – Theme: Unlock the Mysteries

Scripture: "But as it is written, Eye hath not seen, nor ear heard, neither have entered into the heart of man, the things which God hath prepared for them that love him. But God hath revealed *them* unto us by his Spirit: for the Spirit searcheth all things, yea, the deep things of God." 1 Corinthians 2:9-10

Hymn: "Anthem: Hallelujah"

Thought for Today:

As a child around Christmas time I would be excited when gifts were placed under the Christmas tree by family and friends. You could call me "Curious Paul" because I would look at the gifts with my name on it, wondering what was on the inside. Uncertain about the content, I would also shake the boxes to hear what might be inside. Oh, but on Christmas day, what joy filled my heart to see what was inside of the boxes.

Likewise, in our faith walk with God, it takes patience and spiritual maturity to see what God has for us. The gift of God's creative glory is inside of you. So ask God to open up the fulfillment of your destiny inside of you.

Prayer:

Dear God,

Let me abide in You daily, knowing the acts of Your grace and mercy. For You would not come down off the cross to save Yourself but You, with all power, decided freely to buy our pardon. It is a mystery to me why You loved us so. In Jesus' name we pray, Amen.

Reflections:

Other Books by Heart Thoughts Publishing

Intensive Faith Therapy – Vanessa Collins
The Promises of Jesus – Vanessa Collins
The Promises of God – Vanessa Collins
Transcending Greatness – Lawrence Perkins
Lil Fella's Big Dream – Lawrence Perkins
One Way – Dorsey Howard
A Healing Conversation – Edgar Gosa

Visit us at **www.HeartThoughtsPublishing.com**
Or email us at
Info@HeartThoughtsPublishing.com

Made in the USA
Charleston, SC
19 October 2013